# MORTGAGES

## 12 Truths About Home Buying You'll Never Learn From a Bank

The OTHER side of the COIN®

**ALSO AVAILABLE IN THIS SERIES BY WILL DUFFY:**

*Compound Interest: 10 Financial Truths to Protect Your Wealth*

*Mortgages: 12 Truths About Home Buying You'll Never Learn From a Bank*

# The OTHER side of the COIN®

## MORTGAGES

12 Truths About Home Buying
You'll Never Learn From a Bank

**Will Duffy,** ChFC

**Mortgages**
12 Truths About Home Buying
You'll Never Learn From a Bank



OtherSideOfTheCoin.com

First Edition

Includes bibliographical references.

ISBN-13:978-1539710271
ISBN-10:1539710270

I. Business—Investing II. Duffy, Will III. Title

Cover design by Brad Haima, CircleGraphics.ca

Interior design & typesetting by Colleen Sheehan, WDRBookdesign.com

# CONTENTS

**FOREWORD** .......... 9
**PREFACE** TO THE OTHER SIDE OF THE COIN® SERIES .......... 11
**INTRODUCTION:** HOUSE VS. HOME .......... 15
**1.** RENTING VS. OWNING .......... 17
**2.** BUYING A HOUSE .......... 19
**3.** LOST OPPORTUNITY COST .......... 21
**4.** CASH VS. FINANCE .......... 27
**5.** THE TAX DEDUCTION .......... 35
**6.** EARNING A SPREAD .......... 37
**7.** FINANCE VS. FINANCE .......... 41
**8.** 30-YEAR TERM VS. 15-YEAR TERM .......... 43
**9.** SECURITY .......... 49
**10.** FORECLOSURE .......... 61
**11.** DOWN PAYMENT .......... 65
**12.** EXTRA PRINCIPAL PAYMENTS .......... 73
**13.** JACK AND JILL – A STORY .......... 77

# FOREWORD

**MORTGAGES PLAY** a crucial part in most people's financial plans. As Will Duffy so brilliantly expresses, acting wisely when it comes to mortgages requires that you consider the impact of your choices on all aspects of your financial strategy. To do otherwise is simply reckless.

With the stakes so high when you're buying your home, knowledge really is power. If you follow conventional wisdom, at some point you will very likely regret your choices. What you don't know really can hurt you—both in threatening your finances as well as your peace of mind.

After 32 years as a lender, I can attest that not all mortgages are equal. As in most industries, financial institutions sometimes create products that benefit them more than their customers.

Do yourself a huge favor. Before you shop for a mortgage, arm yourself with the true wisdom that Will Duffy has packed into this concise, clear, and comprehensive book. Then you can go out with confidence and find the mortgage that's best for you.

David Ruch
Founder, Nationwide Home Loans, Inc.
September 9, 2016

PREFACE

# WHAT JUST AIN'T SO

*"It ain't what you don't know that gets you in trouble. It's what you know for sure that just ain't so."*
*—Mark Twain*

MARK TWAIN could have been speaking about financial security and retirement when he made those remarks. As a financial advisor, it's painful for me to see how many people accept as gospel all kinds of so-called truths that, in Twain's words, "just ain't so."

Bad information consistently flows from a wide variety of seemingly reputable sources, including some widely recognized financial authorities as well as major financial institutions and government agencies.

Within the world of big finance, a host of interests and motivations influences the distribution of information. Even if each of these interests operates with the best intentions, their messages become distorted by a handful of persistent myths.

In some areas of life, myths may be quaint and harmless. But financial security isn't one of them. When it comes time to retire, learning you'd put your trust in widely held truths "that just ain't so" would be devastating.

I've seen this devastation up close, and it's heartbreaking.

James, a man in his late fifties, came into my office. He was clearly distressed. I asked him what's going on.

"I'm looking at this Retirement Readiness Report you prepared for me, and something's wrong. You're telling me my 401(K), which has a balance of $1 million, will provide only $30,000 per year for us to live on. I don't believe it. It can't be right!"

I reminded him that at retirement, the entire 401(K)—both contributions and gains—is subject to federal and state income taxes.

Before I could continue, James jumped in. "It still doesn't add up. I maxed out my 401(K) contributions at work for most of my career. When I had to withdraw funds for a couple emergencies, I paid back every cent to my 401(K). I thought I was doing all the right things. The rate of return was pretty good most of the time. What went wrong?"

He looked down at the floor. "I don't know what I'm going to do. We can't live on this. We just can't. There goes the lake home. And so much for travel to Europe and New Zealand. And what about the grandkids? I always dreamed we'd be able to help them with college." James dropped his head into his hands. "How did I let this happen?"

As James and I sat there in silence, I thought, *How does this keep happening to people like James? These are good people who are trying to be responsible with their finances.*

Our first impulse on hearing sad stories like James's is to assume they're an isolated case. We really don't want to face this horrible truth: Today it's more the exception than the rule that

**TODAY IT'S MORE THE EXCEPTION THAN THE RULE THAT PEOPLE HAVE AMPLE SAVINGS AND WILL ONE DAY BE ABLE TO RETIRE COMFORTABLY—OR EVEN RETIRE AT ALL.**

people have ample savings and will one day be able to retire comfortably—or even retire at all.

Let that sink in and you'll realize you can't wait another day to separate the fantasy from reality when it comes to your financial security.

In this series, I cut to the chase on the subjects that matter most to your financial wellbeing. These lessons and insights have turned things around for my clients—and I'm confident they'll make a difference for you as well.

If you're willing to consider the other side of the coin, the truth really will set you free.

INTRODUCTION

# HOUSE VS. HOME

*"Home is a place you grow up wanting to leave,*
*and grow old wanting to get back to."*
*—John Ed Pearce*

**HOMEOWNERSHIP** is part of the American Dream. Purchasing a house worth hundreds of thousands of dollars—despite not having that much cash—is a reality. Hence, the American Dream.

I better stop real quick, because something subtle just happened. Did you notice the two words I used to describe where you and your family dwell? I first made reference to owning a *home,* then in the next sentence changed it to *house.* Is a house a home? Is a home a house? This is quite subjective, but I want you to know where I'm coming from. A house is not always a home, and a home is not always a house.

What is a house? A house is a building, consisting of materials such as two by fours, drywall, and shingles. What, then, is a home? A home is where someone lives, where memories are made. As the old saying goes, home is where the heart is.

What we discuss in this book will be houses. The value of a home cannot be calculated. Homes possess immeasurable worth. Instead, we will take a close look at the monetary costs of purchasing the physical structure that surrounds a home. This might be a house, a townhouse, or a condominium. Opinions vary widely on how to handle these costs. It's one of the most misunderstood issues in America today. We'll start with whether it's best to rent or to buy.

ONE

# RENTING VS. OWNING

©Glasbergen
glasbergen.com

**"All we want is a cozy little cottage with a charming rose garden and a white picket fence, six bedrooms, eight bathrooms, a private tennis court and in-ground swimming pool for less than we're paying now in rent."**

**I WON'T SPEND** a lot of time on this because this book is about mortgages, and there is no mortgage when you rent … at least for the renter. But the landlord, the property owner, likely has a mortgage. And guess who's paying it? That's right, the renter. And will the landlord be content to have his tenant simply cover the cost of his mortgage? Of course not. He also wants positive cash flow. So he'll charge rent that exceeds his monthly mortgage payment.

## FINANCIAL TRUTH #1:

### ANYONE WHO RENTS IS RENTING FROM SOMEONE WHO OWNS.

When we understand this simple principle, the whole renting vs. owning debate falls into perspective. When someone is renting a place of residence, they are renting from a person who owns the real estate. And that owner is not in it to lose money. They are renting out the property as an investment, not a charity.

I'm not saying that no one should ever rent. There is a time and place to rent in everyone's unique story. When my wife and I got married in 2005, I was 22 and she was 21. We had both still been living in our childhood homes and needed a place our new family could call home. We didn't yet have the cash for a down payment—or the income to qualify for a loan. And we hadn't yet built the credit scores to get a decent interest rate. So we signed a one-year lease and made a two-bedroom apartment in Englewood, Colorado, our home.

During that first year, the light bulb came on. I realized that someone owned the apartment I was renting. I decided I wanted to be on the other side of that equation. It just made good financial sense. Then one day I got home from work and found a piece of paper attached to the door. It was our new monthly rent charge if we extended our lease another year. And guess what? It was higher! I smiled, crumpled the paper, and tossed it in the trash. I turned to my wife and said, "Let's start packing."

TWO

# BUYING A HOUSE

**"Do you have any other collateral...
besides this e-mail from a Nigerian prince?"**

SO WHAT DOES it take to buy a house? If you don't have hundreds of thousands of dollars in cash, you need three items: income, credit, and a down payment.[1] If you can demonstrate to your bank that you have these, the bank will seriously consider extending a mortgage loan to purchase a house.

1 I'm talking about today. There were times when one could simply state their income, put nothing down and have poor credit—and still purchase a house. This led to a massive wave of foreclosures and short sales, which had a domino effect and contributed to a stock market crash. These NINJA loans [No Income, No Jobs or Assets] were packaged into securities called Mortgage-Backed Securities or Collateralized Debt Obligations. Many of these ended up with little to no worth as people in droves defaulted on their loans.

## WHAT IS A MORTGAGE?

A mortgage is simply a loan used to buy a piece of real estate. This loan is secured by the real estate it's used to purchase. To protect the lender, a lien[2] is placed on the real estate. If the buyer stops making their payments (defaults), the lien gives the lender the right to take back the real estate (foreclose). So a mortgage loan is debt that's collateralized by the real estate it's used to purchase.

## DEBT

Many people hate the D-word, and rightly so. Far too many Americans are buried in debt and can see no light at the end of the tunnel. So is a mortgage bad because it involves debt? No. We cannot lump all debt together and reject it outright. To learn the whole truth about mortgages, we need to look at the specific characteristics of this particular form of debt.

2 A real estate lien is the legal right ensured to the holder of the lien to a specified amount of money upon the sale of the property or until debt owed to the lien holder is paid off.

THREE

# LOST OPPORTUNITY COST

"The bank turned down our loan,
but approved the payments."

## IS THERE A COST IF I PAY CASH?

**READ THE NEXT FEW PARAGRAPHS**, then close your eyes! Imagine you have $350,000 in your bank. You've been saving for years with the goal of buying your dream house—with cash. The day has arrived! You've finally accumulated enough cash to buy the house—with no bank, no debt, and no 30 years of interest payments.

You close on the house quickly because you get to skip underwriting and you opt out of an appraisal. After obtaining the keys, you drive straight to your new house. The love of your life sits in the passenger seat; your children giggle in the backseat. You pull up in your new driveway. Everyone piles out of the car and runs to the front door. They stare at your hand as you insert the key.

As the door swings open, the kids run past and you look at your spouse and smile. "Honey, we did it. $350,000 cash and not a penny more. We'll never have a mortgage payment, never pay interest to a bank. As of today, we will never have a finance cost on this house for the rest of our lives."

Sounds amazing. Can't you just picture the good feelings if that scenario became a reality? Maybe that situation has already been real for you and you've experienced a situation like that. Well, I have a question. That excited claim, "We will never have a finance cost for the rest of our lives." Is this really true? It's an intriguing question. And the answer is even more interesting: It's false.

Don't believe me? Let's keep going.

## YOUR OVERLOOKED COST

Here is one of the most important financial truths everyone should understand: We continually face a subtle but real cost in our lives, often referred to as *opportunity cost* or *lost opportunity cost.*[3] This cost is as real as the day is long. An *opportunity cost* is the loss of potential gain from other alternatives when one alternative is chosen. More simply, when you choose one option (such as paying cash for a $350,000 house), you lose any potential gain from other choices.

3 In this book, I will use the terms opportunity cost and lost opportunity cost interchangeably. I also discuss lost opportunity cost, or LOC, in my first book in *The Other Side of the Coin®* series, *Compound Interest: 10 Financial Truths to Protect Your Wealth.*

What is an alternative in this situation? How about investing the $350,000? That's one possibility. I'm not saying that lost opportunity cost is the final decision maker. I'm just saying it *is* a cost. A *real* cost. And before you can enter a transaction fully informed, all real costs need to be understood.

### FINANCIAL TRUTH #2:

### YOU FINANCE EVERYTHING YOU BUY. YOU EITHER PAY INTEREST OR LOSE INTEREST.

### THERE IS NO OTHER OPTION.

Financial Truth #2 is a bold statement. But it's a fact—an extremely important fact. Let me clarify with an example of buying a vehicle. Let's say the vehicle costs $20,000. If you finance it by getting an auto loan, what is the cost? In its simplest form, the cost is the interest you pay on the loan. By the time you pay it off, you will have paid the price of the car ($20,000) *plus* interest. I think we all understand how this cost works.

If you pay cash for the vehicle, what is the cost? Many people will claim there's no cost because there's no interest. But that's not accurate. While there's no *interest* cost, a cost still exists: the *Lost Opportunity Cost or LOC.*

**WE CONTINUALLY FACE A SUBTLE BUT REAL COST IN OUR LIVES, OFTEN REFERRED TO AS LOST OPPORTUNITY COST.**

In this example, the LOC of paying cash for the car is whatever you could have earned on that $20,000 had you not paid it to the seller. What could you have earned on that amount? Assuming you could have earned *something* on your $20,000, those potential earnings are your LOC.

People don't understand this real cost as clearly as they understand paying interest on a car loan. We feel one cost and not the other. We feel the interest charge because we get a bill each month with it listed. And we see it leave our account and enrich someone else.

Since LOC doesn't hit us in such a tangible way, we tend to forget it's a genuine cost. I'll throw out a silly idea to make a point. Imagine if you received a statement each month after you paid cash for a vehicle. And that statement listed, in a dollar figure, the interest you had lost because you paid cash. Would you feel the cost then? I think so!

Now let's up the ante. Imagine if the bank sent you a statement each month stating how much interest they earned on your $20,000! How would you feel then? You might look back at the amortization schedule they provided for financing the vehicle and wonder if you made the right decision.

Now that we've established there is a cost to paying cash—just as there's a cost to financing—which is lower? There's no one-size-fits-all answer. It depends on the specifics of the decision.

If you're earning 0.50% interest on your $20,000 at the bank and the auto loan charges 12% interest, paying cash is likely the better choice. But if you were earning 10% interest on your $20,000 and the auto loan was 5.00%, it might be a different story. Neither paying cash nor financing is always right or always wrong. It all depends on the specific details.

FOUR

# CASH VS. FINANCE

"The key to home buying is LOCATION. You'll need the money located in your savings account, you'll need the money located in your checking account, you'll need the money located under your sofa cushions..."

**LET'S RETURN** to our discussion on buying a house. This section will assume that someone can pay cash. In that case, is it better to pay in full or to finance? Let's dive into the circumstances of buying a house today. As I write this in 2016, mortgage rates remain at an all-time low.

I just refinanced my primary residence, and my new loan is a 30-year fixed mortgage with an interest rate of 3.75%. I tried to research the history of mortgage rates and found it an impossible task. The rates for 30-year mortgages were not tracked until

NEITHER PAYING CASH NOR FINANCING IS ALWAYS RIGHT OR ALWAYS WRONG.

1971, and 15-year mortgages have been tracked only since 1991. But I did find some data from the National Bureau of Economic Research, which shed light on the history of mortgage rates.

As best I can tell, mortgage rates have never been this low—especially on a 30-year note. Around 1945, mortgage rates dropped below 4.50%, but stayed above 4.00%. I have no evidence that any 30-year mortgage has ever been in the 3.xx percentage range until the past few years. So clearly, mortgage rates are at an all-time low.

Does this factor into our decision to pay cash or to finance? You bet it does! First and foremost, this is an extremely low interest cost. Second, this interest rate is fixed, meaning it cannot increase for 30 years.[4] Thirty years! Is the ability to lock in the lowest mortgage rate in history—for 30 years—a benefit? Absolutely. To put a dollar figure on the interest cost of a mortgage, let's calculate the actual numbers.

The total interest paid on a $350,000, 30-year mortgage[5] at a rate of 3.75% would be $233,526.[6] This means you would pay the lender both the $350,000 principal and $230,000 interest, for a total of $580,000.

That's the biggest reason people hate mortgages and want to pay cash for their house. Who wants to shell out to a bank an additional $230,000? That's a lot of money! Who wants to pay $580,000 for a house that's worth only $350,000?

4 On a fixed-rate mortgage.
5 This assumes $0 down. I will cover down payments later in this book.
6 Hereafter $233,526 will be rounded to $230,000.

**BEFORE WE DECIDE IT'S CRAZY TO PAY AN ADDITIONAL $230,000 TO A BANK, LET'S LOOK AT THE LOST OPPORTUNITY COST.**

Before we get too emotionally involved, let's remember we've calculated only the first cost, the interest. Before we decide that no one in their right mind would ever voluntarily pay an additional $230,000 to a bank, let's look at the other cost, the lost opportunity cost.

We're examining a scenario where someone has $350,000 to pay cash for a house. And we've calculated the cost of financing over 30 years as a whopping $230,000. But what would be the cost of paying cash? What dollar figure represents the LOC? This is more difficult to calculate because we must determine what interest rate someone could earn on their $350,000 if they invested that money instead of using it to pay cash for the house.

To prevent an apples-to-oranges comparison, I'll use the same rate as the mortgage: 3.75%. With these variables identical, it eliminates the chance I'm stacking the deck against paying cash. I'm also using an extremely conservative interest rate. (If you don't think you can earn 3.75% interest on your money, you need new investments or a new financial advisor!)

To calculate the lost opportunity cost on paying cash for the house in this example, we need a compound interest calculator.[7] Feel free to check my calculations. On your compound interest calculator, insert $350,000 in the box for present value (sometimes called *current principal*). Make sure you have $0 in the next

7 All calculations in this book were made with Truth Concepts calculators, which can be purchased at TruthConcepts.com.

box, which represents additions to the principal. We will not be adding any money to the $350,000 for the 30 years. In the next box, input 3.75% for the annual interest rate. Finally, enter 30 for the duration of this calculation in years, as seen in Figure 1.

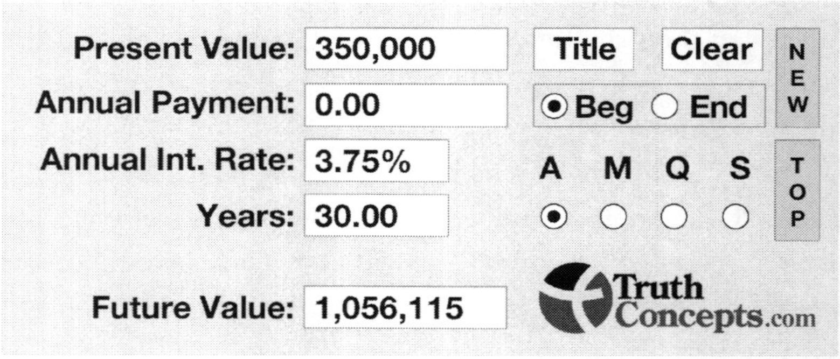


*Figure 1*

FINANCIAL TRUTH #3:

**IT'S BETTER TO FINANCE THAN PAY CASH FOR A HOUSE, IF YOU CAN EARN THE SAME OR HIGHER INTEREST THAN YOU'RE PAYING ON THE MORTGAGE.**

Your eyes are not deceiving you. The value of that 30-year investment is really more than one million dollars ($1,056,115). Since you're likely scratching your head, let's recap this scenario. You have $350,000 in your bank account. You've decided to pay cash for a new house. And you've calculated the interest you'd have to pay if you financed the house with a mortgage.

Over the term of the loan, a 30-year mortgage with a fixed interest of 3.75% would cost you approximately $230,000 in interest. But by reading this book, you've correctly realized there's also a cost to paying cash. So you calculate that cost—and the result is over one million dollars. Which decision carries the higher cost: paying cash or financing?

Before we continue, I must acknowledge that some readers will cry foul. They'll correctly point out that if they pay cash for the $350,000 house, they won't have a mortgage payment. And without a mortgage payment, they'll have extra cash flow to invest. Technically, this is correct. So before we move on, let's consider two crucial points.

## THIS WILL NEVER HAPPEN

The first point concerns human nature. Remember the story of the couple opening the front door of the house for which they just paid cash? Imagine this is how the story continues. They walk through the front door and see the kids running through the unfurnished house. After the wife gives her husband a hug, he walks briskly past her into the kitchen.

She follows, curious why he's in such a rush. When she turns the corner, she sees he's opened his laptop and typed in his password. She asks, "Hon, what are you doing?"

He looks up at her. "Babe, time is of the essence. Remember how we didn't want a mortgage? Well, it turns out the only way the decision to pay cash will be advantageous is if I calculate what our mortgage payment would have been—and we save and invest that much every month. I need to find an online mortgage amortization calculator to figure out what our monthly payment would have been. We need to start saving *today*."

She looks puzzled. Not having a mortgage payment was supposed to be less stressful and give them more cash each month to enjoy life. But now it sounds like they'll be burdened with the equivalent of a mortgage payment, anyway.

His fingers type furiously. "I've got it!" he says. "If we save *and* invest $1,620.90 every month, our decision was the right choice. Let me log into our bank account real quick and transfer the money out of our checking account..."

You can't really imagine that, can you? It's crazy talk! How many times has this happened in the history of people buying houses with cash? Let's round to the closest number: *zero*. It simply doesn't happen. People do not calculate what some phantom mortgage payment would have been, then save that amount every month for thirty years.

## CONSIDER THE SPREAD

That was my first crucial point, and here's the second. So far we've discussed the lost opportunity cost at the same interest rate as the mortgage. But what if there's a spread? What if the investments earn a higher rate than the interest on the mortgage? I won't give you the numbers now, because I'll examine them in a later chapter. But I will tell you this: The numbers aren't even close.

So now that we've calculated both costs—financing and lost opportunity—which decision in this example carries the greater cost? Clearly there's a greater cost to paying cash. It carries a cost, in the form of a lost opportunity to invest, of over a million dollars.[8] That makes the $230,000 of mortgage interest feel like pennies on the dollar.

For this particular example, I boldly claim it would be better to get a 30-year mortgage at 3.75% interest and invest the $350,000 for 30 years. That means you pay the lender $230,000 of interest in exchange for the opportunity to invest your own money, earn just 3.75% interest, and turn it into more than one million dollars. Sounds like a no-brainer! It's just good math.

8 At 3.75% compound interest. For more on how to earn true, uninterrupted compound interest, see my first book in *The Other Side of the Coin®* series, *Compound Interest: 10 Financial Truths to Protect Your Wealth.*

FIVE

# THE TAX DEDUCTION

**"And they lived happily ever after until they received the property tax bill for their castle."**

**BESIDES WHAT WE** just covered, are there any other significant differences between paying cash and financing? Yes, there's another *big* difference: a tax deduction. Do you get any type of tax deduction for paying cash for a house? Nope. But if you finance, you get the ever-popular mortgage interest deduction.

As old as the federal income tax, the mortgage interest deduction was written into the tax code to encourage homeownership,

ALL THINGS BEING EQUAL, SOMEONE WHO PAYS CASH FOR THEIR HOUSE WILL PAY MORE IN TAXES THAN ONE WHO FINANCES.

which lies at the heart of the American Dream. This deduction, in its most basic form, is the ability to deduct the interest paid on first and second mortgages on a principal residence or second home. While there are some restrictions that go beyond the scope of this book, generally you can write off the interest on your mortgage(s) when you file your annual tax return.[9] Is this a good thing? I'd say so!

### FINANCIAL TRUTH #4:

### THE TAX DEDUCTION FOR CARRYING A MORTGAGE IS A GOOD THING.

So in addition to the million dollars created by financing for 30 years at 3.75% and investing our $350,000 at 3.75% for that time, there is also a tax benefit for not paying cash. That tips the scales even more toward financing. The addition of tax savings makes the benefit even greater. All things being equal, someone who pays cash for their house will pay more in taxes than one who finances.

9 Also beyond the scope of this book, but important to note, is that the mortgage interest tax deduction may also lead to the ability to deduct the real estate taxes on the property. Without the mortgage interest deduction, it's likely the property taxes would also not be deductible.

SIX

# EARNING A SPREAD

"I've had a 17% mortgage since 1981. I thought about refinancing at 3.5% but I'm waiting for it to go lower."

**WHAT HAPPENS** if you can earn a higher interest rate on the money you invest than the interest rate on the mortgage? (This is commonly referred to as a spread.) Let's calculate the numbers. But first, I want to make something clear. You should never invest money set aside to pay cash for a house in a financial vehicle that could lose money. If you have a mortgage on your home, that's especially risky. The chance of losing your house to foreclosure—and the damage that would inflict on your family—far outweighs any monetary benefit. Today there are many financial vehicles that offer a guarantee of principal, and others that also guarantee growth. There is no need to gamble with your money. That would simply be unwise.

What do the numbers say if we can earn a spread? We already know the cost of the $350,000, 30-year mortgage: $230,000 in interest. We also know that if we earn just 3.75% on our $350,000 for 30 years, it will grow to over one million dollars. So let's calculate what happens if we earn more on our investments than the 3.75% we're paying on a mortgage. I'll be ultra-conservative here for two reasons. First, to show that even conservative rates of return have a large financial impact. Second, to hammer home that it's not necessary to bet on risky investments.

I'll use an investment rate of return of 5.00%, so our spread on the 3.75% mortgage is 1.25 percentage points. Since *1.25 percentage points* doesn't really tell us anything, let's look at an actual dollar figure. Open your compound interest calculator and enter $350,000 under present value. Annual payment will still be $0. The duration will again be 30 years. But this time, input 5.00% as the interest rate, as seen in Figure 2.

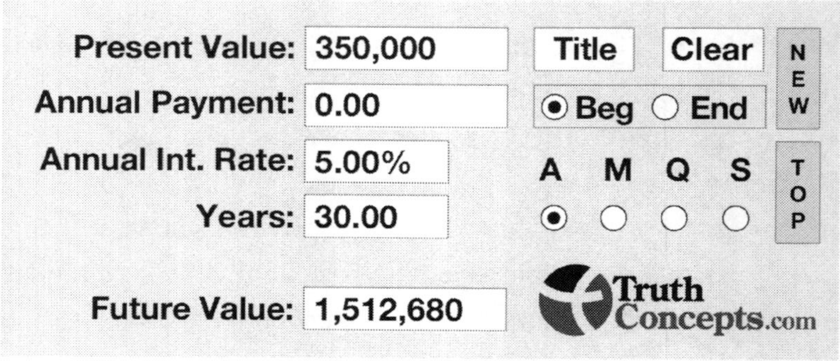


*Figure 2*

The value after 30 years will be more than 1.5 million dollars—that's a lot of money! And if the spread increases, the future value will show a corresponding increase.

### FINANCIAL TRUTH #5:

**IF YOU CAN EARN A SPREAD ABOVE THE MORTGAGE INTEREST RATE, THE BENEFIT TO FINANCING INCREASES SIGNIFICANTLY.**

In an earlier chapter we saw that after 30 years, earning just 3.75% on our $350,000 would result in over one million dollars. Now with a spread of just 1.25 percentage points, we have increased our ending account value by more than 40%. That means an additional $450,000 for you.

I hope you're excited by what you've learned so far. And in case you're thinking, *None of this applies to me—I don't have the money to pay cash for a house!* hang in there. The next chapter is just for you. And it's just as exciting.

# FINANCE VS. FINANCE

**"As an alternative to the traditional 30-year mortgage, we also offer an interest-only mortgage, balloon mortgage, reverse mortgage, upside down mortgage, inside out mortgage, loop-de-loop mortgage, and the spinning double axel mortgage with a triple lutz."**

TO THIS POINT we've discussed only the pros and cons of paying cash vs. financing. But most people can't pay cash. So what are their options? Finance or ... finance!

It's time to dissect the different mortgage options. If your only choice is to finance, you'll want to weigh your options and choose the mortgage that's best for you and your family.

## WEIGH YOUR OPTIONS AND CHOOSE THE MORTGAGE OPTION THAT'S BEST FOR YOU AND YOUR FAMILY.

There are many types of mortgages. There are fixed-rate and variable-rate mortgages. There are conventional and FHA mortgages. There are long-term and short-term mortgages. The list seems endless.

I'd rather not bore you (or myself) by discussing the ins and outs of all the different types. Instead, in the next chapter I'll discuss the two most-popular mortgages: the 30-year fixed-rate mortgage and the 15-year fixed-rate mortgage.

EIGHT

# 30-YEAR TERM VS. 15-YEAR TERM

**"You have been approved for a fixed-rate mortgage. That means if interest rates go up again and you're not paying enough, we'll fix it."**

I'VE HEARD MANY debates on which mortgage is better, the 30-year or the 15-year. Let's settle the debate about the difference between these options. Their name says it all. One mortgage has 360 payments over 30 years. The other has 180 payments over 15 years. Naturally, a 15-year monthly mortgage payment will be higher because the principal must be repaid in half the time.

Most people argue in favor of a 15-year mortgage because they believe that less time means less interest. That sounds reasonable, but let's crunch the numbers. We'll stick with our $350,000 house purchase. But this time there's relatively little cash in the bank, so financing is our only option. Which is the better financial decision: 30 years or 15 years?

In addition to the difference in duration, right off the bat there's a difference between these two mortgages. And that's the interest rate. The 15-year mortgage has a lower rate.

Remember how I just refinanced, and my new 30-year mortgage has an interest rate of 3.75%? Had I decided on a 15-year mortgage, my interest rate would have been just 3.00%, a full 20% lower. So now we have half the duration and a much lower interest rate. Surely a 15-year mortgage is the better decision, right? Let's take a look.

To come as close as we can to an apples-to-apples comparison, we need to run these calculations for 30 years. We can't run one calculation for 30 years and the other for only 15. So unless otherwise noted, every calculation in this section will be over a 30-year period.

We've already calculated a $350,000 mortgage at 3.75% over 30 years and discovered it would cost $230,000 in interest. A 15-year mortgage for the same principal but a 3.00% interest rate would cost just $85,066 in interest. That's $148,000 less. So does that make the 15-year mortgage the obvious choice? You're right, we still need to calculate the LOC!

The lost opportunity cost in this example comes from the difference between the two payments. The monthly payment for the 30-year mortgage is $1,621. But the monthly payment for the 15-year mortgage, even with its interest rate of only 3.00%, is $2,417. That's an additional $796 each month.[10]

10 Hereafter, $796 will be rounded to $800.

**CALCULATE THE COST OF SENDING THAT ADDITIONAL MONEY TO THE MORTGAGE COMPANY EACH MONTH, INSTEAD OF KEEPING AND INVESTING IT.**

If you opt for the 15-year mortgage, that means you're prepared to shell out for your house payment $2,417 per month. And if you're trying to decide between the 30-year mortgage and the 15-year, calculate the lost opportunity cost of sending that additional $800 to the mortgage company each month, instead of keeping and investing it.

This is similar to the question of paying cash vs. financing. Money can be used to purchase the house in a shorter time to avoid paying extra interest—or it can be held back and invested.

To keep things fair, let's start by comparing just the first 15 years. At the end of that time, the 30-year mortgage will be halfway complete and the 15-year mortgage will be paid off. So we'll compare where you'd be if you chose the 30-year mortgage and invested the $800 each month at 3.75% (the same interest rate as the 30-year mortgage) vs. choosing the 15-year mortgage and making no investment.

## WITH A 15-YEAR MORTGAGE

At the end of 15 years, this mortgage would be paid off. But how much money would have been invested? In this example it would be $0. All of the $2,417 monthly payment went to the mortgage company to avoid paying the extra $148,000 in interest on the 30-year mortgage.

For someone who chooses a 15-year mortgage, this isn't necessarily a bad place. You may not have any money invested, but think of all the interest you'll now save by having no mortgage. I'm guessing that at this point, you're curious about what the numbers will be for the 30-year mortgage. I am, too.

## WITH A 30-YEAR MORTGAGE

Again we find ourselves at the end of 15 years, with the 30-year mortgage only halfway finished. But $800 per month has been saved and invested at 3.75%, the same rate as the mortgage. How much money has accumulated in these first 15 years? As seen in Figure 3,[11] the number has grown from $0 to $193,503.

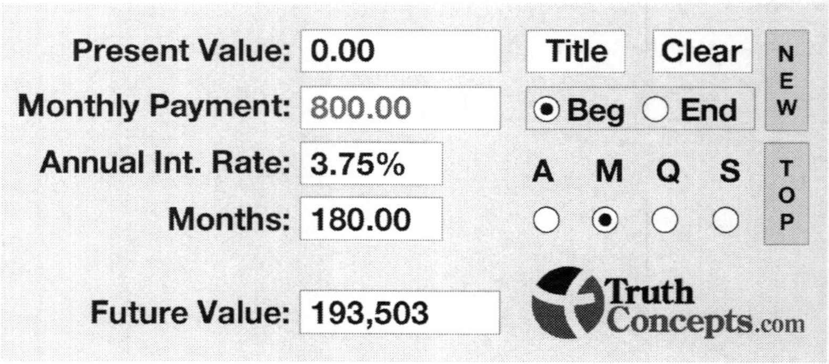


*Figure 3*

That's almost $200,000—certainly not chump change. But does this difference alone—almost $200,000 invested vs. $0 invested—mean the 30-year mortgage is better? Not yet. We've

11 This is a monthly calculation and 180 is the number of months in 15 years.

covered only 15 years. For this to be an accurate comparison, we need to look at the entire 30-year period. But first we'll consider some consequences that mortgage-holders face when they encounter an emergency.

NINE

# SECURITY

"We're offering you an assumable mortgage. We assume you'll make the payments and you can assume we'll make your life miserable if you don't."

**BEFORE WE LOOK** at the second 15 years, I need to point out a critically important consideration. Which of these scenarios, the 30-year mortgage or the 15-year, provides more security when life happens? In which scenario could you better handle an emergency? The clear winner is the 30-year mortgage.

PEOPLE TALK ABOUT SIX-MONTH EMERGENCY FUNDS. THIS IS A 60-MONTH EMERGENCY FUND!

## IF YOU LOST YOUR JOB

Let's consider some common emergencies. Imagine you were laid off—eight years into your mortgage. It can happen to anyone.

Where would you find yourself if you had the 30-year mortgage? You would still be responsible to come up with $1,621 each month to make your mortgage obligation. How will you do that without any income?

Remember, you have been saving $800 per month. And after eight years, that $800 per month has grown at 3.75% interest to $89,682. Do you think you can cover $1,621 each month with almost $90,000 in your accounts? Easily. In fact (assuming the remaining balance still grows at 3.75%), you could make over five years of mortgage payments with that money. I hear people talk about six-month emergency funds. This is a 60-month emergency fund!

But where would you be if you lost your job eight years into a 15-year mortgage? The circumstances are far less favorable. Instead of having to come up with $1,621 each month, your monthly obligation is $2,417. That's 50% higher! And to make matters worse, you don't have any savings. That $2,417 each month is a huge chunk of money when you've just lost your income.

Will you lose your house? You probably will. But to what lengths would you go to avoid losing it? I know I'd do everything I could! So you'd likely take the first job you could find. It might not be one you enjoy. It might not pay what you're worth. But to save your house and all the equity you've built with eight years of mortgage payments ... you don't have much choice.

### FINANCIAL TRUTH #6:

**YOU HAVE MORE FINANCIAL SECURITY WITH A 30-YEAR MORTGAGE BECAUSE THE MONEY SAVED FROM NOT HAVING A HIGHER MONTHLY PAYMENT CAN SERVE AS AN EMERGENCY FUND.**

Think about what happened in the situation I just described. This isn't something we could calculate mathematically, but what is the cost of taking a job you loathe—at lower pay than you deserve? What is the LOC on your emotional health of going to work every day to a place you dread? What is the LOC of taking a job that pays you less than you're worth—when you could have held out for a better job at better pay, like a person with a 30-year mortgage?

These are extremely significant factors. The lost opportunity cost, not to mention the psychological costs, could easily be in the hundreds of thousands of dollars, or even millions.

WHAT IS THE LOC ON YOUR EMOTIONAL HEALTH OF GOING TO WORK EVERY DAY TO A PLACE YOU DREAD?

## LESSER EMERGENCIES

Losing your job is a huge life event. But what if something less drastic happened? Let's say your vehicle breaks down and the cost of repair is so expensive, it makes more sense to buy a replacement. You need to spend $20,000 quickly so you can simply drive to work each day. You and your spouse carpool to get through the week, but that weekend you must purchase another car. Where will you come up with the $20,000?

## SAVINGS OR DEBT?

Time and again I see people who are financially strapped by the high payment on their 15-year mortgage. It keeps them from saving. When they financed their house, they were sure that once they got that mortgage paid off, they'd be able to save. Unfortunately, this is the exception. And what will they do until their mortgage is paid?

Might you need a new vehicle in the next 15 years? That's highly likely. But with the 15-year mortgage, you still have $0 saved. Given that situation, what do most people do? That's right, they finance the car. I once met someone who actually bought a car on a credit card. Yikes!

## DEBT'S DOWNSIDES

Going into debt in this kind of situation has multiple costs. The first is obvious: the interest owed to a financial institution. But there are many less-obvious costs. Will someone who finances a vehicle spend more than if they paid cash? I've seen it over and over again. Once they make the decision to finance, they buy way more vehicle than they need. It's human nature.

Financing feels like we're spending someone else's money, and that gives us a different mindset. (Ever wondered why the government has a spending problem?) Spending too much money on a vehicle, simply because a financial institution (poised to profit from your loan) says you can is not the best financial decision.

There are still more costs. How about the LOC on the interest? How about the closing costs on the auto loan? How about the fees if you're late on a monthly payment? The list goes on and on.

I need to make a crucial point real quick, in case you're thinking you can beat the system by getting 0% financing on a vehicle. The interest on that loan was built into the purchase price. Banks are in the business of making money. And they've come up with incredible marketing tools to convince us to help them take more of our money. The "0% loan" is one of their best inventions. (I've fallen prey to this one, too.)

My mentor Bryan Bloom, who wrote *Confessions of a CPA*, explained to me that the interest is built into the car's price. If you don't take the 0% loan and instead pay cash, they will sell you the car at a lower price. The difference between those two prices is the hidden interest charge.

There is yet one more cost that also can't be calculated: debt's slippery slope. What is the cost of going into debt that first time? Of using a credit card to finance a purchase that first time? Of getting an auto loan that first time?

Sadly, many people fall into debt and can never climb back out. Using a credit card to finance is so easy and feels so good. How does the old saying go? Short term pleasure creates long term pain.

Once someone spends too much with their first auto loan, they may feel they deserve that car they can't afford. Then every time they need a new vehicle, they repeat the mistake. So the financing continues. The debt continues. So many Americans have become slaves to their debt, working harder and harder just to get out of the red.

## MYTHS OF MORTGAGE BURNING

Let's return to our storyline. Though it's a best-case scenario, let's assume the person who chose the 15-year mortgage was able to pay it off in 15 years. He accomplished this without ever going further into debt and was never without income. Now he can save a lot of money without a mortgage payment. But did he make the best decision with the 15-year mortgage?

Again human nature rears its head. Many well-intentioned folks have planned to pay off their mortgage in 15 years, then planned to continue to save the same amount each month as their old mortgage payment.

But you know what they say about good intentions. How many people actually follow through? I'm sure some have gotten off to a good start. If their 15-year mortgage payment was $2,417 per month, they began putting that $2,417 into their savings or investments each month. But how many continue to do so for the

MANY WELL-INTENTIONED FOLKS HAVE PLANNED TO PAY OFF THEIR MORTGAGE IN 15 YEARS, THEN PLANNED TO CONTINUE TO SAVE THE SAME AMOUNT EACH MONTH.

next 180 months? I suspect that number bears a striking resemblance to zero.

You've heard of mortgage-burning parties. Why do people throw those parties? Is it to celebrate that they still need to transfer the same amount each month from their checking account? Hardly. It's to celebrate their freedom from that obligation. It's to celebrate that their standard of living can now improve because they will have more money each month to do fun things.

In case there's someone who actually paid off their 15-year mortgage, then saved that same amount for the next 15 years, let's look at the numbers. (I don't mean to slight anyone who accomplished that feat. If you're out there, good job!) We're crunching these numbers to help those who are trying to decide between a 15-year mortgage and a 30-year mortgage, so they can make the best decision.

## 15- VS. 30-YEAR

The inputs on our compound interest calculator will change a bit. This time for the present value, we will enter $0. That's because we do not have the ability to pay cash for the house. The monthly payment into our savings will be $800 for the 30-year mortgage.

Let me explain where this number comes from. The purchaser is trying to decide between a 30-year and 15-year mortgage. The monthly payment for a 30-year mortgage on a $350,000 house at 3.75% is $1,621. The monthly payment for a 15-year mortgage on a $350,000 house at 3.00% is $2,417. The difference between those two numbers is $800. That's the amount we will save each month if we choose the 30-year mortgage. And saving this much is definitely doable! (Much more so than $2,417 each month.)

After entering $800 as the monthly payment, enter 5.00% as the interest rate and 360 months as the duration, as seen in Figure 4.

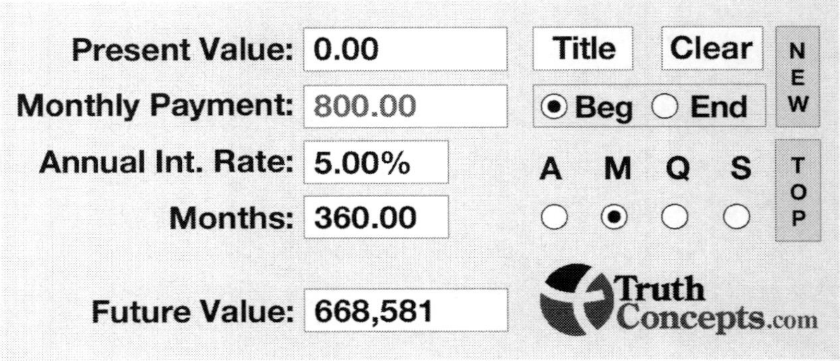


*Figure 4*

Saving $800 per month for 30 years at 5.00% will give you $668,581. For comparison's sake, we will calculate the highly improbable situation that someone who saves $0 for 15 years suddenly acquires the discipline to save $2,417 per month for the next 15 years. Despite how unlikely this is, let's look at the result.

As you can see in Figure 5, the two differences in our calculations will be our monthly payment and our duration. The monthly payment (into our savings) is $2,417. And the duration is only 180 months.

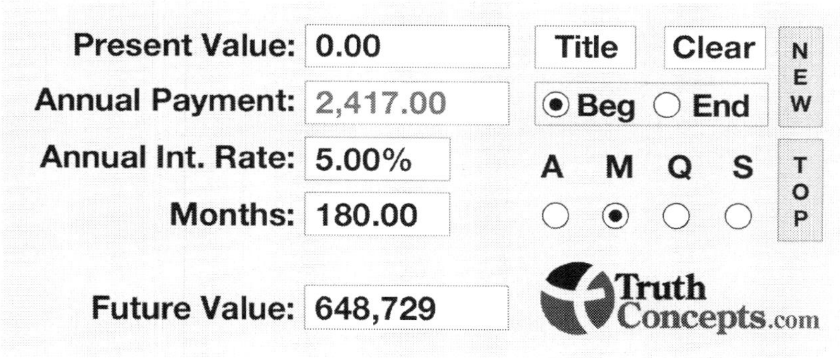


*Figure 5*

This number is close to the 30-year mortgage saving, only about $20,000 short. So what does this tell us? First and foremost, there is practically no difference between these two strategies: saving $800 per month for 30 years or attempting to save $2,417 per month for 15 years. And if there's very little difference in the result, which option is better?

### FINANCIAL TRUTH #7:

### YOU'LL HAVE MORE MONEY IN THE END WITH A 30-YEAR MORTGAGE, EVEN COMPARED TO CHOOSING THE 15-YEAR MORTGAGE AND SAVING THAT ENTIRE PAYMENT FOR 15 YEARS AFTER IT'S PAID OFF.

Clearly the 30-year mortgage is the better choice—for many reasons:

- First, you end up with more money. (And that's based on a 5.00% return. With a higher rate, the spread increases. At 7.00%, the spread grows from $20,000 to over $200,000.)

- Second, the 30-year mortgage gives you more tax savings via the mortgage interest deduction.

- Third, you have liquidity for the first 15 years. This enables you to take advantage of investment opportunities, handle emergencies, and avoid the risk of going into debt, losing your house, or settling for a less-than-ideal job.

- Last, the odds are much more favorable for you to follow through with saving $800 per month than having the discipline to save $2,417 per month for 15 years.

Personally, I don't think there's an argument for the 15-year mortgage. As we've just seen, the numbers will never end up on its side. The only argument I can anticipate is a protection against foreclosure. A 15-year mortgage puts you on a path to escape the risk of foreclosure twice as quickly. As soon as the 15-year mortgage is paid off, the danger of foreclosure is gone, while the 30-year mortgage extends this risk for an additional 15 years. Is this a valid argument? Let's take a look in the next chapter.

TEN

# FORECLOSURE

**"We might hang on a bit longer if we get a second mortgage on our house, the dog's house, the bird house and Barbie's house."**

## THE RISKS OF 15 VS. 30

**DOES A 15-YEAR MORTGAGE** reduce your chances of foreclosure? I'll argue it doesn't. Instead, a 15-year mortgage *increases* your chances of foreclosure.

As I've said, banks are in business to make money. And they can make money when they foreclose on a property. They actually *try* to make money on a foreclosure. And if there's no money to be made, they may not foreclose! I know someone who lived in their house for seven years without ever making their mortgage payment—and the bank didn't foreclose. How could that happen?

The bank views a potential foreclosure as a financial decision that will result in either a profit or a loss. They consider several variables: the approximate value of the property, the remaining debt on the property (the balance on the mortgage), and the condition of the property.

These make for a neat calculation to help the bank determine if foreclosing will be a smart financial move. So if you've ever met someone who didn't make their mortgage payments and wasn't foreclosed, you can bet they owed more than the property was worth.

On the flipside, sometimes the bank may be poised to foreclose as fast as the law allows. I was once involved with a private school in Arvada, Colorado, and privy to their financial statements. The property was worth about $7 million, and their mortgage balance was about $3 million. When the school's attendance dropped, they could no longer make their mortgage payment.

So would the bank want to foreclose? Absolutely! If they foreclose and can sell the property for $7 million, that's a cool $4 million gain for the bank. They'll take that any day!

The school recognized this and knew they couldn't afford to miss a single payment. The risk was too large—$4 million too large. So they obtained private, high-interest financing, just to make the mortgage payment. They bit the bullet on this until they could sell the property. And that's exactly what they did.

## FINANCIAL TRUTH #8:

## THE MORE EQUITY YOU HAVE, THE GREATER YOUR CHANCES OF BEING FORECLOSED ON.

Think about this. I know it sounds backwards. Someone who is upside-down on their house (owes more than it's worth) has a lesser risk of being foreclosed than someone with a lot of equity. That doesn't seem right, but that's how it is.

How do people end up in either predicament? The Smiths get a $0 down-payment loan. When their house drops in value, they stop making mortgage payments. They end up under water and might not be foreclosed on.

But the Wilsons make a large down payment, say 20%, and get a 15-year mortgage. They sign up for the bank's bi-weekly payment program, which accelerates their loan payoff. They build equity so fast, they become a potential foreclosure target!

Have you ever wondered why the banks are so quick to offer their bi-weekly mortgage payment program? As soon as you buy a house, the bank calls to tell you that if you sign up for this bi-weekly program, you could save tens, even hundreds of thousands of dollars in interest.

Wait just a minute. The bank is calling to tell you a way to prevent them from getting all of this interest money you owe? Something's fishy. The bank is not going to volunteer information to help you beat them out of money.

> A SIMPLE RULE I TEACH MY CLIENTS: DON'T DO WHAT THE BANKS TELL YOU TO DO. DO WHAT THE BANKS DO.

The answer is simple. Your equity benefits the bank. The faster you build equity, the sooner risk is transferred from the bank to the property owner.

There is a simple rule I teach my clients: Don't do what the banks tell you to do. Do what the banks do. So when the bank offers you a bi-weekly payment program, know immediately that this benefits them—and not you. And just say no.

The same goes for when the bank tries to entice you to sign a 15-year mortgage with a lower interest rate than the 30-year mortgage. This also benefits them, not you.

ELEVEN

# DOWN PAYMENT

"Do you still offer those mortgages with hardly any money down, super low rates and no payments unless you threaten me?"

## LESS OR MORE?

**IF EQUITY TRANSFERS** risk off the bank and onto us as homeowners, what does this mean for making a down payment? Almost everyone has been told that with down payments, the bigger the better. But as I've already done in this book a few times, I'll disagree with traditional thinking.

There are many downsides to making a big down payment. Before I cover them, let's discuss if there are any advantages. I can think of only one: to avoid something called PMI[12] or private mortgage insurance.

In America today, mortgage insurance is required on all FHA loans.[13] For many, this insurance will last for the duration of the loan, perhaps 30 years. For this reason, I seldom recommend an FHA loan. Sometimes an FHA loan can't be avoided. But if you are able to choose between FHA and conventional, I recommend conventional.

When is private mortgage insurance required on a conventional loan? It's required when the down payment is less than 20% of the purchase price. Going back to our example, 20% of a $350,000 house purchase would be $70,000. That's a lot of money! So does PMI mean someone should put 20% down if at all possible? The answer, believe it or not, is still no. This brings us to the disadvantage of making a large down payment.

Again, we are discussing costs—specifically the cost of private mortgage insurance. To cover all bases, we need to look at the lost opportunity cost when a large down payment is used to avoid PMI.

Let's calculate the LOC of putting $70,000 down on a $350,000 house purchase to avoid private mortgage insurance. We'll need our compound interest calculator again. Enter $70,000 as the present value. And enter $0 for the annual payment. Again use 5% for the interest rate and 30 years as the duration, as seen in Figure 6.

12 This is also known as LMI, Lenders Mortgage Insurance.

13 For up-to-date information on FHA loans, see www.fha.com/fha_requirements_mortgage_insurance

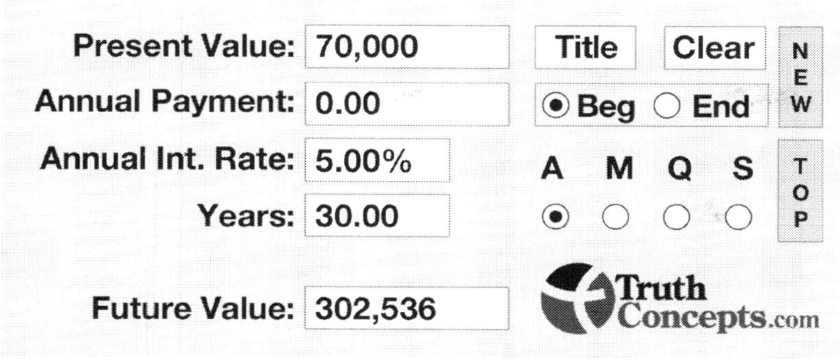


*Figure 6*

As you can see, the lost opportunity cost for putting $70,000 down is a whopping $302,536.[14] That's not chump change! Is the LOC of more than $300,000 worth avoiding private mortgage insurance? Absolutely not.

## FINANCIAL TRUTH #9:

**THE LOST OPPORTUNITY COST OF A LARGE DOWN PAYMENT MEANS IT'S NOT ALWAYS THE BEST DECISION TO AVOID PRIVATE MORTGAGE INSURANCE.**

If a $70,000 down payment costs us over $300,000, what will PMI cost us? There's no easy answer. For starters, it's based on many variables. Credit score, type of loan, duration of loan, and size of down payment all factor into the cost. While I cannot give you a precise answer, I can confidently tell you it's nowhere near $300,000.

14 Hereafter, $302,536 will be rounded to $300,000.

When it comes to paying PMI, many homebuyers don't know there are options. (Sadly, these options also seem a mystery to many mortgage loan officers.) PMI is usually paid monthly. It's built into the mortgage payment and can be seen as one of the line items on a mortgage statement.

But many people don't realize PMI does not have to be paid monthly. It can be paid upfront[15] at closing in the form of a one-time fee. And the one-time fee is much less expensive than monthly PMI. Why? Because monthly PMI is actually the one-time PMI financed at a very high rate—sometimes higher than a credit card!

Because I understand lost opportunity cost, when I purchased my current house I opted to pay PMI instead of putting 20% down. Because I also opted to pay it upfront, it was less than $4,000! The number may not be that low for everyone. But $4,000 is a mere fraction of the lost opportunity cost of over $300,000 by putting $70,000 down on a $350,000 house purchase to avoid private mortgage insurance.[16]

If at this point you think I'm crazy, I won't hold it against you. I know this book challenges almost all the conventional wisdom about buying a house. But it's mostly simple math. And math does not lie.

The reason this book series is called *The Other Side of the Coin®* is because I want to educate people that there are alternatives when it comes to financial products and investing. As you have seen, the other side of the coin for mortgages has a tremendous financial impact in your favor.

15 This is not referring to the upfront PMI on an FHA loan. FHA loans have both an upfront PMI and monthly PMI, neither of which can be avoided. Yet another reason I prefer conventional loans.

## THE BIGGEST COST

Now that we've taken care of PMI, let's look at the other cons of making a large down payment. The biggest cost? You guessed it: lost opportunity cost. This will be much like our discussion on paying cash vs. financing, but on a smaller scale. Let's look at the difference between putting 5% down[17] and 20% down.

On a $350,000 house purchase, we've already seen that a 20% down payment would be $70,000. A 5% down payment would be just $17,500. To determine which is better, we need to calculate two things: the difference in the cost of the mortgage and the LOC of the larger down payment.

If someone purchased a $350,000 house with 5% down, they would end up with a mortgage payment (principal and interest) of $1,540. With 20% down, their payment would be just $1,297. So is the monthly savings of $243 worth putting an additional $52,500 down?

Again, we need to revisit our story and ask ourselves honestly: Will someone who puts 20% down calculate the difference in their mortgage payment had they put only 5% down, then save that amount faithfully each month? This is highly unlikely. I'd venture to guess that almost no one who put 20% down instead of 5% would save the $243 each month for 30 years.

So I'll assume in this calculation that the person who put the 20% down made no special calculations about phantom mortgage payments with 5% down. But I will assume that the one who put only 5% down invested the remaining 15%. That is a more likely

16 Today there is also an option to have the lender pay the PMI. This is known as LPMI, lender-paid mortgage insurance. The lender will pay the upfront mortgage insurance cost in exchange for a slightly higher interest rate. With today's historically low interest rates, this offer can make financial sense.

course of action, especially for someone who takes their money seriously.

If someone has $70,000 to put down on a $350,000 house, but decides to put just 5% down and save the difference, they will have $52,500 to invest. If I calculate how much this $52,500 would grow after 30 years at 5%, it's $226,902, as seen in Figure 7. That's almost a quarter-million dollars!

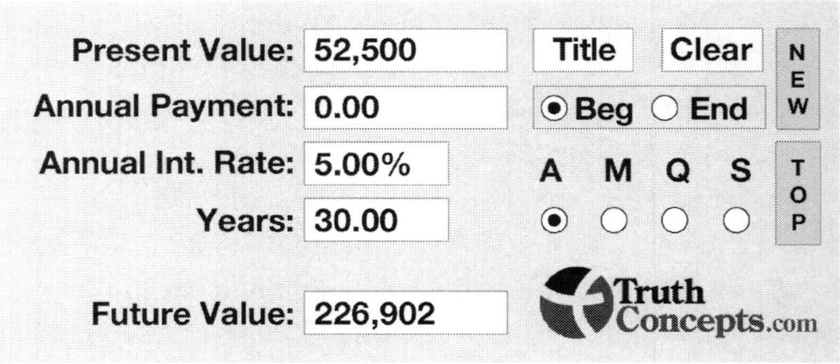


*Figure 7*

## FINANCIAL TRUTH #10:

### A LARGE DOWN PAYMENT LEADS TO A LOST OPPORTUNITY COST THAT COULD EASILY REACH HUNDREDS OF THOUSANDS OF DOLLARS.

So in this case, the lost opportunity cost of putting 20% down, instead of 5%, is nearly a quarter of a million dollars. These are big numbers. Many people don't have $250,000 saved for retirement. But that amount is achievable if someone puts 5% down, instead of 20%, and earns 5% interest on the difference.

17 5% down is approximately the lowest down payment that can currently be made on a conventional loan. There are programs that allow for a smaller down payment, but I want to cover the most popular programs available to the greatest number of people.

## MORE MEANS LESS

The numbers show us that putting less down is a better financial decision. And as we've discussed, it's also safer. The $52,500 withheld from the down payment could serve as an emergency fund to make mortgage payments if a job is lost. And we've also seen how increasing equity transfers risk from the bank to the homeowner.

There are other reasons that I've seen—up close and personal—why large down payments can hurt someone financially. While many people think it's a good idea to make a large down payment to help them afford the monthly mortgage, the dangers are far too common. Let me clarify.

Making a larger down payment reduces the monthly mortgage cost. Some people will make a large down payment, even greater than 20%, to make the monthly payment more affordable. (In some rare cases, this is necessary to meet DTI limitations.[18])

But making a large down payment to reduce the monthly mortgage payment comes with two problems. First, there is a huge lost opportunity cost, which we've seen can reach hundreds of thousands of dollars. In some cases, when someone is trying to use a large down payment to qualify for the mortgage, the LOC can reach or exceed a million dollars.

Second, putting down a large sum to qualify usually means the purchaser is buying too much house for their income. In my opinion, the banks already allow DTI ratios that are too high. Some allow a buyer to have a mortgage payment that's 50% of their gross income. Their mortgage payments alone will cost

18 DTI, debt to income, refers to the limitations imposed by lenders on the amount of debt one can have in relation to their income. It is usually expressed as a percentage. A 50% DTI limit would mean one is limited to having 50% of their gross income to cover debt payments, including their mortgage.

THE NUMBERS SHOW US THAT PUTTING LESS DOWN IS A BETTER FINANCIAL DECISION. AND IT'S ALSO SAFER.

them 50% of what they make—before taxes! That leaves just half of their gross income for everything else.

## NOT TOO BIG

If your house purchase incurs a mortgage payment above 50% of your income—requiring a large down payment to lower the DTI ratio—that house is simply too much for you. A lot of my clients have asked for my recommendation when purchasing a house, so as to not buy too much. My opinion is this: If you have to put more than 5% down to qualify for the mortgage, that's too much house. You should qualify for the mortgage payment with just a 5% down payment.

Making a large down payment to qualify for a mortgage brings unnecessary lost opportunity costs—to the tune of hundreds of thousands of dollars. It could also lead to buying too much house. And that inevitably causes difficulty to meet such a large financial obligation. And those difficulties can lead to foreclosure, stress, and marital tension. It's just not worth it.

TWELVE

# EXTRA PRINCIPAL PAYMENTS

"Of course we can afford it. A $500,000 house with a 30-year mortgage only costs 6¢ a minute!"

**I WANT TO HIT** on another common misconception about mortgages: when someone sends to the lender money beyond the minimum required amount. Someone with a $1,500 mortgage payment might send a check for $1,700, with the extra $200 applied to the principal balance.

The reason for doing this, some argue, is that it reduces the amount of interest ultimately paid on the loan. And it does exactly that. Paying principal ahead of the amortization schedule[19] reduces the overall interest paid. To take an extreme example, if an extra principal payment was made for the entire remaining balance, all future interest payments would be voided.

But as we saw with the 30-year mortgage vs. the 15-year mortgage, the amount of interest due is not the end of the story. Simply knowing you can save interest by making extra principal payments does not give the full picture. LOC must again be factored.

Each time an extra principal payment is made, that money could have been invested. So I must ask: Why would you pay off a mortgage debt of 3.75% any faster than you had to? Can you make 3.75% somewhere else? How about more than 3.75%? And what about the mortgage's tax benefits? Why hasten the end of a good thing?

### FINANCIAL TRUTH #11:

### EXTRA PRINCIPAL PAYMENTS BENEFIT THE BANK, NOT YOU.

## SMILING AT A BAD DEAL

This story will bring home the disadvantages of making extra principal payments. John gets into his car during his lunch break. The sun is shining, and he is smiling. He is going to his local bank. He's smiling because he came into some extra cash. As he always does, he puts the windfall into an extra principal payment on his mortgage.

19 An amortization schedule is a breakdown of each of the principal and interest payments in a given loan. Each payment is the same amount, yet the amount that goes to principal and to interest will change with each payment.

John walks into the bank and sees his favorite teller. They exchange a smile and a wave, and he walks up to her station. When she asks John why he stopped in, he explains he's there to make an extra principal payment on his mortgage.

"Great!" she says. "Let me pull up your account."

As she types away on her computer, John begins pulling out $100 bills—10 of them. He counts them out on the counter and says, "One thousand dollars!"

She slides his money toward her so she can verify his count.

"You guys," John says, "do not owe me any interest on this thousand dollars. As a matter of fact, I'm making my thousand dollars incredibly difficult for me to ever get back. If I'm ever in a time of need, I'll have to come back here and fill out an application[20] to get my money back. I'll cross my fingers that the bank thinks I'm qualified to have my money back. And if they do, I'll take my money on the bank's terms and pay whatever fees they decide to charge me, along with whatever interest rate the bank wants me to pay."

Say what? Who in their right mind would accept such a deal, let alone propose it?

If you've ever made an extra principal payment, you have agreed to that deal. An extra principal payment is money you will never get back—unless you refinance or sell. It can never be invested. It can never bail you out in a time of need. It is, for all intents and purposes, gone.

20 An application would be required, as the only way for James to access the $1,000 he is making in an extra principal payment is by requesting a home equity loan or a home equity line of credit (HELOC).

THIRTEEN

# JACK AND JILL – A STORY

"I knew there was a balloon payment due, but who expects to pay more than five dollars for a balloon?!"

**WE'VE COVERED** a lot of variables. Sometimes it's difficult to put them all together and grasp the cumulative benefit of all the advice of this book. So I'll finish with a story about two co-workers, Jack and Jill.

While their lives are quite parallel, Jack and Jill have very different views on mortgages.

Each is 35 years old. They live in the same neighborhood, across the street from one another. They both built new houses and even picked the same model. They each paid $350,000.

Jack and Jill were surprised to see each other in the orientation class on the first day of their new jobs. As coincidence would have it, their employer assigned Jack and Jill the same positions. Jack covered the West region and Jill covered the East. Since they held the same position, they earned identical salaries.

Jack was a numbers guy. He loved math and spreadsheets. He always had a calculator handy. When he went under contract on his new house, he told the builder he wanted a 15-year mortgage. He proudly said he had 20% saved as a down payment, so he could avoid mortgage insurance. The lender took over from there and initiated a credit check to make sure his credit score was high enough for the loan and that his debt would not exceed a certain percentage of his income.

Jill was carefree and always had a smile. She usually made decisions by instinct with a pinch of logic. When she went under contract on her new house, she told the builder she wanted a 30-year mortgage. She also wanted to know if she would qualify to put just 5% down.

While she had enough to put 20% down, she wanted to maintain an emergency fund in case she ever found herself struggling financially. She wanted to make sure she would never lose her house. The lender started the application process for Jill, checking her credit, debt, and income.

Underwriting went smoothly for both Jack and Jill. They each had W-2 income, which banks like. They both had relatively high paying jobs. Their down payments were easily sourced, and they both had credit scores over 750. Both were quickly approved. Jack emptied his savings account and brought a $70,000 check to closing. It pained him to see that $0 representing his new savings balance, but he was happy to fulfill his goal of putting 20% down.

Jill also had $70,000 in her savings account. But she removed just $17,500 for her down payment, representing 5% of the $350,000 purchase price. Her receipt showed a savings balance of $52,500. This made her feel good, because it was a cushion she could fall back on if needed.

At closing, Jack was shown a Truth-In-Lending statement that detailed his mortgage interest rate and monthly payment. The rate was just 3.00% on his 15-year mortgage, and his monthly payment was $1,934.

Jill also received a Truth-In-Lending statement. Her rate was higher, because it was a 30-year mortgage. Although her rate was 3.75%, her monthly payment was only $1,540. That's almost $400 less than Jack's. And not only was her rate higher, so was her mortgage balance. Jack's 20% down payment brought his balance to $280,000. Jill put just 5% down, so her balance was $332,500.

Despite a higher rate and principal balance, Jill's monthly mortgage payment was still almost $400 less than Jack's—because her 30-year term was twice as long as his.

Jack and Jill closed on the same day. They actually bumped into each other at the title company. Jack had just closed, and Jill was walking in for her closing.

That evening, Jack and Jill sat in their new houses, overwhelmed with joy at now being homeowners. They were both quite responsible and got right down to business thinking about the future and making important financial decisions to ensure they would never lose their new house.

Jack decided to pay off his mortgage even faster than 15 years. So he crunched some numbers and decided he could send an additional $200 each month as extra principal payments. If he sent in $200 extra each month, his mortgage would be paid off almost two years sooner! This really got him excited.

Jill took a different tack. She wanted to make sure not to spend all of her income. Her father had always said, "Your expenses will rise to equal your income. If you ever get a raise, decide how much you want to save from your new income and start doing it immediately. Otherwise your spending will quickly rise to match your income and you'll lose the ability to save." Before she received her first paycheck, Jill decided to save 10% of her net (after-tax) income, which came to $7,200 per year, or $600 per month.

So Jack's monthly mortgage payment was $400 higher than Jill's—plus, he was sending an extra principal payment of $200 each month. Jill's mortgage payment was $400 less than Jack's, and she was saving $600 each month toward her retirement. This makes their monthly outlay identical. Jack was spending $400 more on his mortgage, and Jill was saving that same $400. Jill was depositing an additional $200 each month into her savings plan. Jack's version of a savings plan was to put the same $200 into extra principal payments to pay off his mortgage sooner, before beginning to save.

JACK'S VERSION OF A SAVINGS PLAN WAS TO PUT $200 INTO EXTRA PRINCIPAL PAYMENTS TO PAY OFF HIS MORTGAGE SOONER.

It's important to note that Jill would be adding $600 each month to the $52,500 that remained in her account after she withdrew just $17,500 for her down payment. Jack's account would remain at $0, because his $200 extra each month was going to the bank, not into his savings account.

Jill felt at ease with her decision, went to bed, and drifted contentedly off to sleep. Jack was confident in his number crunching. While he was a little uneasy about having no money in the bank, he convinced himself it was a sacrifice worthy of the reward. He could see the light at the end of the tunnel. And as soon as he paid off his 15-year mortgage, he would start saving like crazy.

The chart below shows where Jack and Jill started on Day 1 in their new house.

DAY 1

| JACK | JILL |
|---|---|
| 15-year mortgage at 3.00% | 30-year mortgage at 3.75% |
| $1,934 monthly payment | $1,540 monthly payment |
| $200 extra monthly principal payment | $0 extra monthly payment |
| $0 in savings | $52,500 in savings |
| $0 added to savings each month | $600 added to savings each month |

Let's fast-forward five years and check on Jack and Jill. Everything has gone according to plan. Jack has not missed sending $200 each month to his lender, on top of his required payment. Jill has continued to add $600 each month to her account. But her money is no longer sitting in the bank. She found a safe, liquid vehicle for her money, where she earns 5% annual interest. She thought this was much better than earning just 0.50% at the bank.

END OF YEAR 5

| JACK: 40 years old | JILL: 40 years old |
|---|---|
| 15-year mortgage at 3.00% | 30-year mortgage at 3.75% |
| $1,934 monthly payment | $1,540 monthly payment |
| $200 extra monthly principal payment | $0 extra monthly payment |
| $0 in savings | $108,779 in savings |
| $0 added to savings each month | $600 added to savings each month |

Notice the only change? Jill's savings increased dramatically. She went from $52,500 to $108,779. Jack's numbers all stayed the same because his savings of $200 each month goes to the bank and not into his account.

Now let's fast-forward to the end of year eight and check again on Jack and Jill—because misfortune is about to strike them both.

END OF YEAR 8

| JACK: 43 years old | JILL: 43 years old |
|---|---|
| 15-year mortgage at 3.00% | 30-year mortgage at 3.75% |
| $1,934 monthly payment | $1,540 monthly payment |
| $200 extra monthly principal payment | $0 extra monthly payment |
| $0 in savings | $149,758 in savings |
| $0 added to savings each month | $600 added to savings each month |

Jack has no money in the bank, but he has crossed the halfway point for paying off his mortgage. Jill still has 22 years before her mortgage is paid, but she has amassed almost $150,000 in savings.

At the end of year eight, the economy takes a dive and the whole country feels the pain, including Jack and Jill's employer. Both get a pink slip.

Jack is left with only three options. The first is to find a job immediately—even one he dislikes and that pays poorly—to continue making his $1,934 monthly mortgage payment. The second is to sell the house, although that can take time and is subject to the market in a depressed economy. While selling will relieve Jack of his monthly mortgage obligation, he will suffer a substantial loss as his house is now worth much less than he paid for it.

Jack's third and worst option is foreclosure. But he may not have a choice. If he can't scrape together almost $2,000 each month to make his payment, the bank will probably foreclose. Remember, he has built a ton of equity. His 15-year mortgage builds equity twice as fast as a 30-year mortgage. Plus, he has been making extra principal payments of $200 each month for eight full years (96 months). Due to his substantial equity, the bank could make a small profit by foreclosing on Jack. The only one to lose money here would be Jack.

(Don't worry. I won't have the bank foreclose on him. We'll return to Jack in a moment to see how he escapes disaster. But first let's quickly check on Jill.)

Jill is disappointed that she lost her job, but she needn't lose any sleep. She has almost $150,000 in savings. And her mortgage payment is only $1,540 per month. She is in no danger of losing her house.

But Jack is really stressed, as he has no good options. He goes online and fills out applications like crazy, hoping to secure some sort of employment before his next mortgage payment falls due. He gets a few interviews, but no job offers yet. His next payment comes due and he calls the bank to ask if they will work with him. Let's consider their conversation.

> *"Thank you for calling ABC Bank, how may I help you?"*
>
> *"Can I speak to the mortgage department?"*
>
> *"Please hold."*
>
> *"Thank you for calling ABC Bank, how may I help you?"*
>
> *"I recently lost my job ..."*
>
> *"I'm so sorry to hear that."*

*"It's been rough, but I'm working through it. But I'm going to have a hard time coming up with my mortgage payment this month—and it's due today! If you look at my payment history, you'll see I've been sending in extra principal payments of $200 each month for the last eight years. I've never missed. By my calculations, I've made $19,200 in extra principal payments over the last 96 months. Would I be able to skip a payment or two until I start a new job? Surely the extra $19,200 will cover me for a few months, right?"*

*"I'm terribly sorry, but we can't do this. Those extra payments have been applied to your principal balance and cannot be used to make any future payments. Your payment must be received today or you will be deemed in arrears as early as tomorrow. Will you be able to make this payment today?"*

*"I have some cash at home. I always like to keep a couple thousand dollars in my home safe. I'll bring this money to the bank today to make my payment."*

*"That sounds great, Jack. We are open until 5:00 p.m. Thanks for being a customer of ABC Bank."*

That hollow thanks is all Jack will get from the bank. Making your payment on time for eight years, making extra principal payments for eight years, and being a perfect mortgage customer will not relieve you of your monthly obligation. Not even for one payment. Jack is in a real bind.

But Jill is not stressed at all. She's unhappy she lost her job, but excited for what new opportunities might lie ahead. She can be highly selective in applying for a new job. She wants to find something she will enjoy doing and will also pay her what she's worth. She is a valuable prospect after eight years of experience with her previous employer. For Jill, things are looking up.

Meanwhile, Jack emptied his cash emergency fund to make his mortgage payment. Now the pressure increased. He despaired about how he could make his next payment in 30 days. As he contemplated his dire situation, the phone rang. It was one of his job prospects, requesting a second interview. Jack became cautiously optimistic.

When Jack went in for his second interview, they really liked him and offered him a position. But it entailed a 20% pay cut, the hours were less than ideal, and it meant a longer commute. Still, Jack had no choice. He agreed to start the next Monday.

Over the weekend, Jack reevaluated his finances. He would no longer be able to send an extra $200 each month toward his mortgage. But that was okay, as he would still have his house paid off in less than seven more years. He went online and canceled his automatic $200 per month extra payment. Then he headed for bed.

Jill did a few interviews, but none of the jobs really suited her. The employers were interested, but she wasn't quite ready to pull the trigger. She wanted to make sure she got a job that was right for her.

A few days later, she received a call on a job she was really hoping for. She aced the interview, and they offered her the position. But when they offered less money than she had been making, she politely said, "I appreciate the offer, but I really need to maintain my income."

The two executives excused themselves and stepped across the hall. Not two minutes later, they returned and told Jill they would match her previous salary. Jill shook their hands and agreed to start the next Monday.

Jack and Jill are now both employed again. Jack's lifestyle will take a hit. He will no longer be able to save in any fashion—not even extra principal payments. But he feels okay because he can again see light at the end of the tunnel. His mortgage will be paid off within seven years.

Jill was thrilled not to have to absorb a reduction in income. She reflected on how valuable it had been to save $600 per month for the past eight years. She did have to tap into her savings to make two mortgage payments during her job search. But because she never felt pressured by her monthly payment, she could wait for the right job. And her account values kept compounding at 5% even though she tapped it to make those two payments.[21] So she suffered no lost opportunity cost on her savings account.

Because Jill did not have to settle for a reduction in pay, she could continue to save $600 each month. She had seen it was worth it. And the $600 she deposited each month grew at 5%.

Happily, no further misfortune befell Jack or Jill. We'll fast-forward six years, which brings us to the end of a 14-year period. Jack's mortgage is fully paid, and he's ready to start saving. He was able to pay off his mortgage a full year early due to his eight years of extra principal payments. Jill is staying consistent and saving $600 each month.

Jack throws a mortgage-burning party. When Jill receives his invitation, it gets her thinking: *Could I pay off my mortgage right*

21 For more on the power of this powerful financial strategy, see my first book in *The Other Side of the Coin®* series, *Compound Interest: 10 Financial Truths to Protect Your Wealth.*

END OF YEAR 14

| JACK: 49 years old | JILL: 49 years old |
|---|---|
| No more mortgage | 30-year mortgage at 3.75% |
| No monthly payment | $1,540 monthly payment |
| $0 extra monthly payment | $0 extra monthly payment |
| $0 in savings | $252,112 in savings |
| $0 added to savings each month | $600 added to savings each month |

*now, with the money I have in savings?* She logged into her bank account to check her mortgage balance. To her shock, she owes only $222,072! Not only could she pay off her mortgage, she could have done so at the end of 13 years. That's a full year sooner than Jack, who had a 15-year mortgage *and* accelerated his mortgage with eight years of extra principal payments.

But as she thinks it through, she has no desire to pay it in full. She is happy earning a spread between the cost of her mortgage and her savings account. She also enjoys the tax benefits of writing off her mortgage interest. (Jack just lost this deduction by completing the payoff.) So she decides to keep doing what she has done for 14 years. And in a sense, her mortgage is also paid off because she has the liquidity to pay it off at any time. The only difference: She is in control of her money and is earning interest on it, instead of the bank.

Jack sleeps in the next morning after his mortgage-burning party. He wakes up with a smile, because today he gets to crunch numbers and begin saving for retirement. After breakfast he strolls into his office and boots up the computer.

He begins thinking about how much per month he wants to set aside for savings. His first thought is to save the same amount as his mortgage payment, $1,934. But it dawns on him how tight things had been financially. So he decides to save $1,500 each month toward retirement.

He feels this is still a substantial amount—and it needs to be since he is now almost 50 and retirement is only about 15 years away. The pressure of reaching the half-century mark with no retirement savings persuades him to bite the bullet and put away $1,500 each month.

Jill stays the course and keeps saving $600 each month, which is less than half of Jack's savings plan. Can Jill keep up?

Fast forward another 16 years. Jack and Jill are now 65. Though human nature would keep most people from saving $1,500 each month for 16 years, Jack exercised great discipline and never missed a month. His savings earned 5% compound interest. Jill continued to save $600 each month, though her income slowly

SHE IS IN CONTROL OF HER MONEY AND EARNING INTEREST ON IT, INSTEAD OF THE BANK.

increased over the 15 years. She used the extra income to treat herself to a slightly better lifestyle.

END OF YEAR 30

| JACK: 65 years old | JILL: 65 years old |
|---|---|
| No more mortgage | No more mortgage |
| No monthly payment | No monthly payment |
| $0 extra monthly payment | $0 extra monthly payment |
| $447,127 in savings | $729,180 in savings |
| $0 added to savings each month | $0 added to savings each month |

Jack and Jill both enter retirement mortgage-free. While Jack amassed an impressive $447,127 in a short time, Jill ended up with almost double for retirement. On top of that, she enjoyed 30 years of reduced tax liability by writing off her mortgage interest. And for 30 years she had the liquidity to handle emergencies and take advantage of investment opportunities.

### FINANCIAL TRUTH #12:

**WHEN IT COMES TO MORTGAGES, CONVENTIONAL WISDOM ALMOST ALWAYS FAVORS THE LENDER MORE THAN THE BORROWER.**

## WHAT WILL YOU DO?

A lot of the traditional thinking about mortgages just does not hold up. We see this from several standpoints:

- Mathematically, there is more money to be made with a longer term mortgage and smaller down payment. The time value of money really shines here. The sooner you can start to save, the better. Don't believe the adage that it's better to pay off your house, then start saving. It simply doesn't add up.

- Essential to any financial plan, there is much greater liquidity in having a smaller mortgage payment and saving the difference. Liquidity gives you the ability to weather the storm in times of financial duress and emergencies. Liquidity also enables you to take advantage of investment opportunities that come your way.

- From a safety standpoint, there is nothing safer than keeping control of your money, rather than using it to pay off your mortgage sooner. A liquid side fund will enable you to make mortgage payments if you incur a reduced income. And the more equity you have, the bigger target you become for bank foreclosure.

A LOT OF THE TRADITIONAL THINKING ABOUT MORTGAGES JUST DOES NOT HOLD UP.

## EQUIPPED TO THRIVE

I hope you have enjoyed looking at the other side of the coin when it comes to mortgages. Look for upcoming books in *The Other Side of the Coin®* series—for more financial truths that can profoundly change your life.

# ABOUT THE AUTHOR

**WILL DUFFY** became a millionaire at age 33 by following the same contrarian wealth-building and tax-saving strategies he teaches his clients. He's the author of the industry-rattling book series *The Other Side of the Coin®*, which includes the eye-opening *Compound Interest: 10 Financial Truths to Protect Your Wealth.* He has earned high praise from legends such as IRA expert Ed Slott, who wrote that book's foreword.

After attending The Ohio State University and receiving his Chartered Financial Consultant designation from The American College of Financial Services, Will dedicated his work to countering the lies, half-truths, and faulty math that prevent millions of people from realizing their wealth potential.

Chances are, you are unknowingly and unnecessarily losing money to financial institutions and the government. You are losing money in investments, fees, and taxes. It need not be this way. Will has helped people retire who thought they couldn't, rescued family estates from tax ruin, and guided millennials on the path to true wealth and prosperity.

Will spends every spare moment he can with his wife and four kids, somewhere in the hills and evergreens near Denver, Colorado.

Visit Will online at:

OtherSideOfTheCoin.com